MYSELF PAINTING

MYSELF PAINTING

CLARENCE MAJOR

POEMS

LOUISIANA STATE UNIVERSITY PRESS

BATON ROUGE

THIS PUBLICATION IS SUPPORTED IN PART BY AN AWARD FROM THE
NATIONAL ENDOWMENT FOR THE ARTS.

NATIONAL
ENDOWMENT
FOR THE ARTS

Published by Louisiana State University Press
Copyright © 2008 by Clarence Major
All rights reserved
Manufactured in the United States of America
FIRST PRINTING

DESIGNER: *Amanda McDonald Scallan*
TYPEFACE: *Whitman, Variator, and Orator Std*
PRINTER AND BINDER: *Thomson-Shore, Inc.*

LIBRARY OF CONGRESS CATALOGING-IN-PUBLICATION DATA
Major, Clarence.
  Myself painting : poems / Clarence Major.
    p. cm.
  ISBN 978-0-8071-3366-8 (alk. paper)
  ISBN 978-0-8071-3367-5 (pbk.: alk. paper)
  I. Title.
  PS3563.A39M97 2009
  811'.54--dc22
                                        2008007398

The paper in this book meets the guidelines for permanence and durabil-
ity of the Committee on Production Guidelines for Book Longevity of the
Council on Library Resources. ∞

For Pamela, with love,
and
in memory of Gus Null,
my first art teacher

CONTENTS

MYSELF PAINTING

[1]

THE RED BENCH

Pier stretches out a quarter-mile into ocean.
At its end this red bench vigorously illuminated,
as if to speak of its purpose. I sit down.
Big morning sky clear and I am small,
grateful and grounded. Yellow oil shimmers
on ocean's hypnotic surface.
Close-cropped morning: presenting itself
as expansive. A slithering profusion:
more than yellow, yellow-orange, yellow-blue.
Purple, too, below a gleaming calmness.
I invite it in where color is needed.
Tides pound shore, leaving spray
standing in mid-air, eye level.
Something overturned,
I feel it, something finished,
something returning to where it started,
to start again.

ART

The glasses are clear.
But how clear is the vision?
If art is an absolute
and a jealous mistress,
then who is responsible
for this juvenile ambition?
Her little fat feet twitch.
Her little fat hands? They sweat.
Save for the view of the ocean—
the gathering clouds waving,
the sheep going down for water,
the moss on the rocks,
the toy sailboat in the nook—
art could be somewhere else.
Perhaps late in the day,
after a snowstorm,
at the edge of the city,
where the last train before dark
is pulling out. It's an absolute
moment but no one is jealous of it.
And kindly with her fat hand
the little girl waves
from the train window,
her glasses fogging up.

TREES

Night or day,
the Sunday painters are all painting
the same motif: the stretch of leaf-clad trees
in sad rows,
tall breathing things panting
in the hot sunlight,
maple or oak, strong or half gone,
things with limbs but no knees or toes,
nevertheless (I see the trees from my moving car)
as alive as I am now
in the test of writing this
on paper not from trees but from garbage,
garbage from the high seas
and backyards of homes and bars.
I simply go where the life of this takes me,
and its motion thrives
as it reaches into the painting of trees
by genteel American women
in the alive countryside.

IN SEARCH OF A MOTIF FOR
EXPRESSIVE FEMALE FIGURATION

She, the many, concentrates with her hand
held in midair, waiting

for the seer in herself. Blue
and naked, love arrives

with a heart half broken,
in a sling, walking on a crutch.

Ponytail. Bare legs.
Summer skirt: young woman on a ladder

painting her ceiling pink.
I stay as if she were land,

new growth everywhere
and a warm bay

pressing her skirt against her thighs.
Everything cut to the bone,

with hands folded in front of her,
just below the belly like an answer

to an unasked question. Nothing
slows her or speeds her tissue thin.

The abating comes.
Her station wagon stands in my driveway,

shadow directly beneath,
and two dogs or call it America,

with a red kitchen table. She bakes, suns,
runs, and rests. Women dancing

on the beach. The girl twins
in a burlap sack together hopping across sand.

She is always a different she.
She moves like she is at the end

of a piece of twine. Spring heat,
winter wheat. Her father in a casket,

a living memory. She, this: mosquito tents,
nets and a dent left in myself

where she once pressed against me.
And the copper kettle's tea

will not completely comfort,
but then I was always crossing

in her headlights, knowing even then
her thighs belonged to her knees

and legs like a train belongs to its rails.
And she could not swim

across the lake of her life
to save her life. I swear.

As she fixed her hair she crossed her legs
and raised her arms

so that her armpits showed hairless.
Beginning blackness. That unbearably lovely arm

extended, color of Tibet sunset,
in a thoughtless Degas gesture. She belongs

to a quiet moment, arabesque all
of its seconds. She stands at the crevice

of the house and the fence, arms crossed
as in self-defense, like when she sits

uneasily in the armchair in north light
wearing a blue bonnet and white stockings,

a gold necklace with a diamond pendant
and lots of bracelets on both arms,

disarming me: my Helga—my Dora,
my Marthe. My Saskia. No surprise,

she comes from memory
of self, a sick girl on her back

in an attic room and her dog
sleeping on the floor beside her bed.

She: I was a gingerbread gypsy
far from reach but now in your colors

I learn to teach myself
my lines, its music—yours.

And through rubble of self my middle
distance is yours too. Pose me, she says,

your gypsy woman with red shawl
draped over one arm, no promise

broken in unchangeable light. Silk.
Swish. Lights overhead blink.

Minus manners on the mezzanine,
leaning over the railing looking down,

we didn't care what people thought
or who saw us use catsup in public

or at the dance school for her daughter
where stumbling girls are amazed

at how long it takes to calculate
correctly unmapped steps

or where knees or elbows go or when
to fold or unfold,

brush stroke after stroke. But
what will break the stalemate?

Or to put it another way: perhaps
two old women coming out

a narrow passageway, carrying straw
baskets of wet laundry balanced

on their heads is the answer—even
to what the wasp, entering a hole

in the old wooden cross high
on the wall above all heads,

wants to know. She defends me,
indefensible as I am, even as the line

dances in my name in celebration
across the surface, rough or smooth,

it's a pagan dance with villagers
gathered round and round, till I find

my way. So secretive! Secrets
keep secrets. This is the image:

scarfed, she is old leaning almost out
of confinement where she lives,

bread basket on arm,
charwoman cut in wood meant to stay,

and I do what I can to hold her
at the table the way I love her,

elbows on table, reading
that same letter over and over

looking up unwittingly, eyes wet,
memory molded to an absence.

And this image: in the dark
theater green, she sings red songs,

whole sad notes meant to be flat-
out joy but are not yet picked up

by washwomen with shopping bags
waiting at bus stops. And like a body

coming up out of Nature she wakes
at daylight, looking at the floor,

her face saying *why* and *what*.
Kitsch figuration?

Not this one, bright-eyed in night
with a flashlight suddenly turned

upon her innocence. Full face, three-
quarters? Sitting or standing or in motion,

turning this or that way? Turned
completely around slowly. Each

limb, line, slope, tested on its quest.
She is sitting in a yard chair, calming

down from the spearing of the day.
She runs, jumps over the pole.

Her shabby genteel gesture unsealed
completely by seamy half-light

and chapel bells ringing a knell.
She strolls bayshore, collar closed

with sparrow clasp, or she sits quietly sewing.
At sea level, she's up again, scarf thrown

over bare shoulders, she finds her way
out into night sand, gazing at antlike stars

and she's left dazed or she's dazzled
by another light: walking the garden,

watering plants. She turns and comes
back this way, sits for my purpose,

bottom of her left foot a face-up spoon.
Fiddle-threaded fingers

through her hair and her twin sister
comes out of my imagination, toes

politely together, two sisters in white dresses,
ribbon-tied and smirking. I can't stop

this or them: her blank mirror looks
back at me, at them, blackly: the girls

and I in a trick mirror. She dances
to the beat of a broken set of dishes,

perfect disharmony, then repose. And pose
must change. Soldiers stepped on

her dance-floor feet—no canteen wallflower
warming a bench-seat. She walks

away, turns and comes back. Sits
quietly, shoulder and arm in a tide

of light, the rest pulled back
in shadows of Hopper's hotel room.

She lies and prides herself on not being
a regular bride. Her den, a dark gold

Rembrandt. She spans the grandstand
as if my trusted brush stroke

bedded us all, knowing life is smarter
than us. From her point of view, one

in this crowd of lace leaps to light
no faster than the next, trying her best

to get through a long sitting. She takes
a straw broom and sweeps the studio floor.

She sits on a cushion and her body's light
fills the canvas, lighting the room,

twin daughters at her sides, holding hands,
skylight light drinking their skin. Gloomy,

with a large hat full of fruit and Matisse
flowers balanced on her head, head

gently rocking like a tree in wind.
The twine of my life, she says,

winds around everything twice. I say,
but surely there must be something

we share besides silverware,
Venetian blinds, pastel highlight. She says

a woman's life is paid in full at birth,
it opens out and it keeps opening

all her life. Heavy-hipped, she walks
slowly up a plank into the shed. A soundless

grayness surrounds her. A gray opening
in me watches her

change, and watches over her
till I finish this, as I finish now.

INTERIOR WITH STILL LIFE

Desire, artichoke green,
holds everything together,

room, table, sunlight coming in.
Shrubbery, personal like a woman,

bending but not breaking.
Desire holds on to even the broken pieces.

Cezanne's green bottles, lilies,
Soutine's paradox of things tilting,

yet not. Slabs of vulgar lunchmeat
on a broken plate. Desire as sunlight

leaves all radiant,
creating the thickness of blue shadows

with cactus green, a budding.
A large bowl of fruit, Russet pears

with rustic personalities.
Gourds, yellow and monumental.

You lift a vase of white lilies and hand it
to the woman who has just entered.

SONG OF CHANCE

Against all dissent, I take a chance
at the game. The rest is talk.
But no matter. This is what I stand for:
random chance. And it's a tight squeeze.
But I stand firm in my effort.
They play a lullaby every time a baby is born
in the ward where you work. And
I'm your bard to appreciate its kindness.
Yet it's all the same, all the same,
because in our fort   otherwise
known as an empire—we deny chance.
You remember, long ago,
I entered my own randomness,
a place in the chance line
at the Saturday night fish fry.
Oh, I took my chances
all right. I took a chance
and came tonight, night of a full moon,
soon descending
when and where everything will matter.
And I am standing here now
longing for you, my lost love,
to take a chance on me,
to join me once again
at this Saturday night's dance
in the frying fumes of catfish,
that sweet and tangy sly fish,
a fish that takes chances every minute
deep in the currents,
currents that dance the light to its own needs.
So, come on back, baby, come on back,
like Lightnin' says, and I promise to be good,
come on back, baby,
take a chance, come back to me,
come on back to me.

PROPAGATION

If botanic roots are divided
and planted,
a profuse spreading happens
but no guarantee;
just as there are not any with her
as she, just for a moment,
has forgotten that she is waiting.
She is looking with a question,
the answer to which is unknown
and no longer matters.
If I let myself love her,
she will take root in me—a garden
already full of adequate
but not remarkable growth.
We are part of something
already parting, multiplying, possessing,
and dispossessing everything we touch.
I say to her, touch me,
hold me—*to hell with everything else.*

QUESTION MARK

In an outfield, but not exactly—more
like a fertile coastal area:
that's the spot, lowland rising
to a forest plateau.
There, I crouched
in this outfield, seeing only the contour
of his body hanging over a tree limb
in the shape of a question mark.
His sadness, his happiness, whatever he was,
all the unknown—possibly unknowable —parts
blended
and long since having left
his flesh like a stream of smoke
leaving a burning car,
long gone out on their own
by now high above pines
mixing with factory smoke.

PATIENCE

The day from noon on shifted
and spread out across the way.
I was diligent in my vigil of the plain.
I stood under a little tree, waiting.
I knew insane traffic
was heavy not far away.
People lining up to see something,
waiting to get into the United
or the Oriental. And she sat
alone in her room somewhere,
chin resting on fist,
elbows on knees,
watchful for nothing in particular.
And the light here under the tree or there
in her room signed its name
as usual on everything it touched,
minute by minute.
And even these trees, reflected
upside down
in the pond here, wave back
with a certain necessary patience.

MY CORNER

By now the view
from the window—with the row
of hotels along the beach,
the sailboats and the tourists in clusters
on the promenade—was a bore.
And this was when my corner
was no longer accessible.
I felt forced to enjoy the chance to stand back
and from across the room
assess the placement of things
replacing me in that corner.
I had to admit they were more interesting
to look at than I myself.
Had I been a painting or a finely carved dresser
or something Rembrandt finished
or did not finish—even something
he'd stopped working on
just in time, so that everything
was left alive—I might have complained.
But as things stood—mortal, and all
the silliness that went with self-interest—
I didn't have a good leg to stand on.

ALL OF US

The elevator was full of black women
in black dresses. A little old white woman
needed reassurance that it was all right
to go up with them. And the nurse's aide
was singing opera in empty hospital rooms,
one after another. At my own pace,
I volunteered to push the trolley
up the track to the zoo.
All the white people were already inside,
and everybody else was in the waiting room.
Is that a woman or a man wearing dogface?
From here you can't tell gender or race.
When I finished, I helped with the elevator.
Everybody needs to be lifted.
Finally, there was dancing in the streets
to angel icons, to gurus. And a naked man
danced with a bear as red and yellow
confetti floated dashingly overhead.
Most of us had a great time.
And even the white people
who forgot whiteness had a smashing time.
But the next morning
the streets had to be cleaned,
so they imported Russian peasants.
And it will take at least
a generation before they finish.

THAT FACE

There is that face
without a tear or *tear*
yet, troubled—or seemingly so,
as if it's had all it can take
but not so bothered really,
really friendly as a bird's nest,
just stuck with the habit
of its familiar scowl, its suspicion,
stuck with its sensitivity, itself, its fear,
with how it's perceived,
often negatively.

But I can still see
that scared boy in it, misunderstood,
and now with his mother's thin hair
after those prime years
of afro, then that office-ready look.
Now all the colors—grays
purples yellows, deep hues—sleep
together in a lulled rubble,
worn as a bit in a brittle horse's mouth.
And I still see that face
with more than a dime's worth of affection.
And she who loves it sees it too.
And there's nothing left to muckrake or toy with.
What seems troubled produces no howl.
The otherness of it, in an odd way, is a thrill.
That's what's left and that's what's good.

TABLE FOR TWO

Night, and we were the only two customers
in the restaurant. And you had to go
all the way through a dark room
to reach light. A custom and a test,
I gather. Sun-drenched,
we rested once there, you and I.
An empty bottle, I'd noticed
on the way in,
stood on the white surface
of a dining table in the dark
by an inner doorway.
Outside, through the big window we saw
what was left of a tested and wrecked ship
moored on the beach. And a nun
on a nearby bench counted rosaries
as children were digging in sand,
as though in search of something
that would surprise everybody.

GATHERINGS

My hands gathered together
on the table,
a gathering of fingers
expressing a staying dance.
Seven men gathered around
two men playing a game
on a board between them
balanced on their knees.
Their gathering trance expresses faith.
The real show dance is green and yellow,
and the landscape of the dance
expresses the confidence of trees
in the rain, sun, snow—the gathered
things of September or anything.
This may be a stage,
or it may be another kind of real place.
A limber group of men
in tights huddled together
like football players,
showing heads whispering together.
Their tight gathering expresses only itself.
It is real and it's a stage
and it's an ongoing dance,
with bright dresses flying out
from thighs and deep cries echoing
out beyond what is known.

COFFEE SHOP

She sees me,
a stranger coming in
in a town where everybody knows
everybody else,
and she pauses in mid-step
holding a coffee cup in one hand
and a steaming coffee pot
in the other. Her mouth
opens slightly,
as if she is about to ask me something,
but she does not;
instead
her face relaxes with a half smile
waiting for me to do or to say—what?
I don't know
because all of her understands
that it is really clear
from my confident stride toward her
clear from the look in my eyes
in themselves question marks
that it is my turn,
as though I owe her an explanation,
and I am sure I do
in this town
or feel that I do.

THREE

She opened the door
to see who'd knocked three times.
It was the maid with her three children.
She said something about the procession
at Three Points. This is the procession
of the three wise men,
and as usual Casper is in third place
because that's where the first three
artists placed him. Actually,
she used her third finger
and the car door was open.
Anybody passing by could see.
And through the window, I see
the front of my car on the other side
parked in the rain on a Paris street.
Well, it could be Paris. Ménage à trois.
You could tell when it's Paris
because the green angel stands
with outstretched arms
and shows no sign of hunger
or anger or angst. And she pulled open
her third eye to fish out the hair irritating it,
while one cluster of my entourage
hovered above us
like heavenly guests
and the other gathered below
around us like calm cattle
at the end of any day.
I gave each of the kids three pieces of candy.
Anyway, it didn't matter
how she later climbed the long stairway
to our hotel room, but as she went up
her dress fell off. It's how they make the clothes
these days—so flimsy. And
St. Sebastian looks up,
as if at her nakedness,

looks with dreamy eyes,
one arrow planted in his neck,
one in his stomach,
and the third in his left thigh.
And in the room just as I take her shawl
from her shoulders,
with her enchanting smell under my nose,
three familiar men gaze in
from outside the window,
waving wrapped gifts
like salesmen in an info commercial.
The driver had parked this way
three cars down and gone into a tabac
to buy cigarettes and that is how it happened,
how I got stuck
and couldn't get across the street
in the rain,
but we were safe now in the room,
at least till morning
though the riots were still going on
in three sections of the city.

KEYS

I keep two separate rings of living keys,
my house key and the mailbox key
are together;
and my office key,
the key to the office building,
the key to the mailroom,
and the key to my wife's office
are together;
and there is another key—
a lone key on a plastic string
that hangs in the garage—
it's the key to the backyard gate.
And then there is in a drawer
a tin can full of dead keys,
keys to doors I no longer open,
keys to cars I no longer own,
keys to back gates I no longer open
to take the garbage cans out.
But the two rings of living keys
I keep with me,
and they have become
extensions of my hands;
they are little silhouettes of possibility,
tested things made to imitate nature,
things designed to ward off suffering,
things of access to the familiar world
of my comforts, my secure lair.
Though small and hard,
they represent not only access
but arrival and accomplishment,
and sweet arrival
and modest accomplishment
stand always for love.

IN LINE

Standing in the prescription line,
the old women complain
about how slow the clerks are.
They can never find prescriptions.
I nod agreement,
not telling them that I keep my expectations low
so that I don't feel the frustration they feel.
I stand there between two of them,
gazing toward the ceiling,
planning my chores for the day,
knowing I need to do something
about the yard and garden
back and front,
knowing I need to do something
about the violets and daisies,
and knowing I need to catch up with Paul
and his love of plants,
catch up with Vincent
and the Japanese artists
and start studying a blade of grass,
really looking at it
till it reveals its many dimensions
and stigmata secrets.
I certainly have plenty of grass front and back,
more than I want front and back,
and I need to study hard
till I understand,
as Walt understood
how it represents all the other plants,
all life all glory front and back,
back and forth throughout time,
and once I can sense
in a blade of grass
the old women complaining about the clerks
not finding their prescriptions
and sense the clerks in their frustration too,

then I will know
the meaning of something
important—never mind being able to explain it,
just sensing it will be enough
but I know I have to be patient—no pun intended.

DOG HOPE

The neighbors' dog,
dragging his rope,
follows me to the mailbox,
as though he expects something good
to happen there. I don't mind him following me,
but I hate to disappoint him.
He looks at my bills
and other junk with such disappointment.
There is nothing good to eat in the mailbox.
I keep telling him that.
I open it and show him.
He looks but is not convinced.
What I say is bunk—obviously.
His sad face is understandable,
but he still has hope.
Each day it's the same thing.
And who knows—one day
something good
may be there.

THE POET'S TREE

The Birch and the Juniper,
like two well-dressed ladies sitting in church,

in our backyard are heavy with rainwater
from erratic rain all night,

yet they will not break, they will shake
off their burden and stand straight,

but our Laurel leans over so far heavy
with rain that I am sure headwinds

will eventually bring it down,
snapping it about midway.

The baking sun is its friend.
May sound trite to say,

it never really had a chance
because of the giant tree in the next yard

crowding its air space.
In that house, first the man died,

then the woman. Now their son rents it out.
He lives across town and rarely comes this way.

THE HOLE

A man out there is digging
a dada hole in the earth
and the question is not so much
what will go into it, birth or death,
but what will come out of it.
Reasons for the seasons
Made holy or unholy?
Balance between volume and shape?
Patches of colorlessness
or bent contours?

The dada hope
is for space symmetry of place.

If not symmetry
between fullness and emptiness,
what will he do
with those tiny patterns of displacement
being released, as we speak,
with each shovel full?

Look, look, there goes one now,
Slightly lopsided, circling his head
like a broken halo.

THE RIFLE

His wife with wet hair
won't go into the forest anymore with him.
No wonder she knows
in her eyes what Mona Lisa thought.
She sits on the back porch
watching him descend into the thicket,
his rifle on his shoulder
pointing to the tops of trees
that have done him no harm.

After their wedding ceremony
he went outside and smoked a cigarette.
For her that was the beginning of the end.

SETTLERS

How will these early settlers decide where to stop
and what to call the new place?
They'll have to clear the land
and cut down those tall trees.

There is the leader by his wagon
surveying the hillside.
Is that a tear running down his cheek?
Weighing losses and gains, figuring
how to abide this bargain or insanity?

Danger is for sure.
It may ride down from those hills,
or emerge from the earth,
or sneak up out of the underbrush.

His whole body, though, says he's ready.

MAP OF THE PARK

A dilapidated park at the edge of the city
was the old woman's favorite place

to read her library books. Years earlier,
when the park was new,

she and her lover often came here.
She now sat on the bench

by the map post
with the book balanced on her lap.

Today her book put her in a trance.
She looked *through* the words

as though they were glass and
was led by them

into the room of a young painter
who had just killed himself

because the woman he loved
rejected him. He was from the projects,

and she was above that.
The old woman leaned over his body

to see if she could revive him.
It was like looking down into a trench.

He smelled of linseed oil.
With her fingers she rigged open this mouth

to see if she could hear breathing,
and instead she recoiled,

seeing an image of her own face
as a young woman looking back at her

as she was at a time
when she loved a young painter

who did not return her love.

CITIES

I was born in a city,
unaware of myself at the time,
then leapfrogged my way—
slightly aware of myself—
through small towns,
then to another city,
and since years have passed
and I am older if not old,
I still can't bring myself
to claim any particular city,
though I know many—Atlanta,
Chicago, New York, Paris,
New Orleans, London, Nice,
San Francisco, Rome, L. A.,
and cities not coming to mind
at the moment, and—unlike Doris
who claims London or Maurice
who claims Paris—I cannot
get an intimate relationship going
with a particular city. Yet
there are any number
of little things and big things
I love about each one,
the way the streetlight shines
a rich yellow at night in one,
and in another the way the noonday
light strikes the tops of certain buildings,
or the way children along the way
from school leap through sprinklers,
or the burst of fireworks on holidays
or noisy colorful parades
in celebration of one thing or another.
So I don't claim cities,
but if one ever tries to claim me
I won't be able to do anything about it.

THE PEACOCK

It was at the San Diego Zoo
near the entrance
that I spotted him
among other impressive peacocks,
on pencil-thin legs strutting his stuff,
with his tiny blue head held high
and with his brightly colored tail
stretched out behind him
like art for art's sake
or some such nonsense.
And I thought
that head—higher than the tail—is
not about a small brain,
rather, it's about balance
with the elaborate design at the rear.
He was saying with his strut—*look at me!*
And by turns he stopped
by the purple Trailing Ice plant,
then by the red Fuchsia,
then by the yellow Zinnia,
and even by the bright dress
of a woman standing close to his fence,
to prove his superiority.
And from across the yard,
Autumn Joy and Dusty Miller
and Chinese Wisteria agreed,
bowing their heads out of respect.

CELL PHONES

I'm worried.
I own a cell phone.
It's in my pocket.
No one has ever called me on it.
I have never heard it ring.
It's always off unless I'm using it.
I haven't used it in say three or four months.
I've been out all morning
driving around Sacramento
running errands.
Sacramento is a city
full of people walking and driving cars,
and more than two thirds
of the people I've seen this morning
walking and driving cars
are talking on cell phones;
even three girls walking
shoulder to shoulder
together in the park
were talking on cell phones,
presumably not to each other.
So, you will understand why
I'm beginning to worry
about myself
and that other one third.
Something is seriously wrong.

CAFÉ LIFE

Many of the people of Paris
live in tiny apartments that are dark,
with no temperature control,
and therefore
they tend to spend
a great deal of their time
out in brightly lighted cafes
with plenty of temperature control.
There is a certain ironic attractiveness to living
much of one's private life in public,
but here we live a different way,
comfort at home is something we cherish.
So two men showed up
first thing Monday morning,
ready to improve our comfort.
Using a ladder one climbed up
through the narrow opening
into our attic where our units are
and where it was a hundred
and twenty-five degrees.
The other handed things up to him
and took things handed down.
They worked hard and sweated.
I liked them;
they were wonderful company.
And after two days we had a new system,
but on the way out the guys said,
"oh, by the way,
when you turn on the furnace
be sure to go out to a café for a while
because the outer surface of the furnace is oiled,
and when it warms you will smell
the nasty smoke
and the smoky smell of oil burning
will make you sick.
The smoke will set off your fire alarm,

so be sure to alert the fire department
and your alarm company
before you do anything—
let them know what you're about to do.
Then go to your favorite café;
cafes can be wonderful places
to hang out,
even to get to know interesting people,
other people with computers,
or someone sketching,
or see old friends you haven't seen in awhile,
and eating out, if you're hungry, is fun, too,
you can order things
you wouldn't think of eating at home,
it can be an interesting way to live,
I mean hanging out in cafes.
So have a coffee, a fancy coffee,
linger there for several hours,
and be sure to take something to read,
a romance novel
or a legal thriller
or a book about dogs or politics,
you have to decide,
or take your computer and hook it up—
you'll feel more at home with your computer—
and you can surf the internet
and just relax and enjoy café life,
and don't worry about the furnace.
The oil will burn off,
and the smell will go away,
and you can come home again.

BLACK OR WHITE

Some members of the family were black,
some white,
and the black ones knew about the white ones,
but the white ones didn't know
about the black ones,
and they lived all over the country,
West Coast East Coast South
and even in Alaska.
She was eighteen and white
when she found out about her black relatives,
and finding out knocked her sideways
and shook the ground under her feet.
So she asked her professor
what makes a person white
and what makes a person black,
and he said it's simply a matter
of what people believe you are
and she still didn't understand.
So she found the black members of her family
and asked them why they were black
and why she was white,
and they said because
that is what everybody believes,
by the old rule of slavery times,
when they wanted lots of free labor,
if you had one drop of us in you
that made you black;
so today if you got one drop of us
left over in you
that makes you one of us,
but if nobody knows about it
you are white,
and she still didn't understand.
So she tried to stop thinking about it,
but awake or in dreams
the question never left her.

So when she met a white boy
she wanted to marry,
she told him she was black,
and he said I don't care,
I love you,
and as far as I'm concerned you are you
because I love you,
and that is all that matters.

BOULDER AND DAVIS

I dreamed I was dreaming—
that it was not a dream but it was—
and in the dream I lived in Boulder
with a woman with brown hair
with the smell of Iowa summer heat still in it.
We lived in a little clapboard house
painted many times red,
and each red was darker than the previous red,
and we were happy there
even when the snow was twenty inches high
at the front door and you couldn't get it open.
On such mornings we stayed in bed anyway
and made love and read books
and ate cheese and tomato sandwiches
made with whole wheat bread
slightly sweet with honey.

In the summer we drove up in the mountains
on narrow roads that scared us both,
and we laughed at our fear.
The months and years passed,
and we traveled abroad and returned,
traveled and returned,
till we finally sold the house
and moved across the country to live
in a town called Davis on a street
that at first had no other houses
then finally two, then three houses.
And at the front door, which faces west,
late in the afternoon the sun baked the door,
sometimes so hot
that you couldn't touch the doorknob,
but it was okay because we went
mostly in and out through the garage.

[2]

SELF PORTRAIT

At the wedding of myself
and the mirror,

You, my best man, say nothing is more dishonest
than a self-portrait done out of love.

So, I *will* to be what I will not be.
I will not shock myself

giving myself St. Dominic's face,
I will not be a lover on a white horse,

I will not be the Minotaur in heat,
a pimp with ten ladies,

an excuse for the human figure elusive and polite,
Rembrandt's brand or Jacob Lawrence's cobwebs

or Kossoff's bodies struggling up out of mud,
or any of those biblical subjects,

big and strong,
bearded saints galore,

I will not be Angry Eyes standing by my easel,
I will not be an old man in a dirty smock.

I will leave the canvas empty till I know
for sure. The empty canvas is about possibility.

THE WEDDING

Paint the wedding with flailing figures
and give the landscape high on a hill

in which the festivities are taking place
something we can *see,* say, the big mouth

of a fish opening,
and let *that* be the sculpted sun.

Then the dancing jumping bride
and the dancing jumping bridegroom may

fall to the buttered grass, giggling,
and guests in black and white are amused.

The city spreads out lazy below,
seen in its sculpted glamour

but too far away to be heard
in its clamor, so let it be—and up here

let the wedding dance itself crazy,
let it strut its stuff

till the wind changes. Call it dream time
or time out, call it what you will,

we need it because we *live* down there.
So, let us dance

till the big mouth of the fish closes.

BY CANDLELIGHT

Imagine an old woman in black
is reading a book by candlelight

to a reclining nude on a bed
who is half asleep

yet she hears the words
through her wet skin

shimmering
in lemon light.

Inside the nude's head
the words turn to images.

Once upon a time, the book says,
there was a young woman

and her grandmother
at the dinner table

and a guitar left
by an unknown person

on the table stood up
and played itself.

The music was otherworldly,
which made it hard

for the young woman eating
supper at the table

to keep her toes from wiggling,
and soon her knees parted

and she was on her feet.
When she looked,

her grandmother had turned
into a handsome young man

shaped like a mandolin
and before long the two of them

were dancing
to the strange score

and begging for more
and more and more.

WHAT PEOPLE SAY

They say there is a fine line
between a mess and a success.

The Greeks say that one hair
from you know where

can launch a thousand ships,
but what can they do to stop the leaks.

Ships far out appear to glow
like glowworms. Gloating, Gauguin said

to his friends let's paint a Cezanne,
with no harm to Cezanne.

The French are known to say hello
and goodbye, in French, of course.

They also say we're very catholic
but not very religious.

The Italians say many things
about politics and the weather

over and over, especially at noon
in small bars in every byway.

Americans? What do American say?
They say they are misunderstood.

VAN GOGH STOLE FIGS

In this garden out of Zola's dream,
Vincent walks quietly among ripe fruit

and bright flowers orange and white
against the brooding darkness

of green cypresses in lust.
The lieutenant walks with him

sharing the figs.
Figs make people sing.

Imagine the two of them
bursting into song.

But is it just a loving glance from someone
or the law of light

or a motif for a scene
that they want? They sing at singing

and even in the dust of the road
they dance at dancing.

But is it the shadow behind the trance
of art that they really want?

Maybe that's it! Maybe that's it. The loop
of art, how it breaks into a circular dance.

That's what Vincent teaches the lieutenant
when he teaches him how to draw,

how to see, how to find the balance,
he says *let it sing, let it dance.*

WINDOWS AND WOMEN

This is Rome where women beat rugs
out windows,

women hang sheets and shirts and shorts
and baby diapers on clotheslines

stretched from window to window,
women and children in daylight in the cobbled

allies between tall buildings
crammed together. Old women

everywhere milling about,
pushing things, lifting things,

carrying things,
going to the hog butcher,

coming back from the market,
scattering the pigeons,

women stopping to talk
with the ragman,

women stopping to talk
with the basket-maker,

women stopping to inspect the goods
of the vendors

at the end of the street.

And in Australia
the Cathedral termite too

stays busy erecting cathedrals
of sand

taller than women,
taller than men,

building
as much as they destroy.

ALLEGIANCE

See me in silhouette
against a stretch of poppies

red atop the greenest green.
Upstairs in the baker's rooms,

golden unicorns plucking apples
from a mile of black trees

around and around the room,
a simple allegiance to what is out here

as far as the eye dares see.

LATE AFTERNOON PICNIC

Looks like rain.
We stop on our way back

from the wedding,
returning the car

to the airport.
In the distance

we see chairs turned backwards
leaning against pine tables.

Nothing could be lonelier.
Summer, too, is over.

With waterfront shops in view,
sitting on grass, we picnic

under two old trees sharing
the same root system.

Weed clusters springing up

to sunlight at our toes,
seeds dropping on our blanket.

Darkness of rain coming
in from the ocean, and soon

shopfronts in the electric night
will sparkle in memory of tourists

who will not return till next summer,
when the soprano will again sing

and the flute player,
waiting for the barefoot girl to dance,

will play softly and quietly,
but we will not be here.

4 AM

Through the front window
the yard's tall trees wave darkly.

As usual the shuttle driver is late
and lost circling the park.

He takes out his map,
it's coming apart at the creases

as his nearly dim flashlight moves
across unclear lines.

At the airport the computers are down,
and the whole place is gripped

by a nervous energy,
yet no one is appalled.

SCRAGS

Evening along the coast
the sea-road leads away

toward a meadow through which a path
winds down to the station

where your train might or might not
arrive on time,

and meanwhile across the way
I watch workers in the scrags

who will work till sunrise.

RED BRICK

Teen boys in blue suits,
blue shirts and blue ties
rolling around on blue grass
and telling each other blue lies
under a good blue sky
after a long hard winter of blues.
No real agenda
till a tall woman
old enough to be their mother,
wearing a mini skirt, tight, red,
crosses the park,
walking so close
they could have reached out
and touched her powerful legs.
She's headed for the street
with a long brick wall.
They gaze,
and from that moment on
no talking. Each boy goes deep
into himself for a visit
to his own unknowable connection
to that woman whose brave shadow
crawls along the wall following her,
just as the boys,
without moving, also follow her.

KIKI'S INTERSECTION

She is in a doorway waiting for the obvious.
No one hates her—yet.

But what is that large feeling that keeps
spreading through the air?

She is now down on the sidewalk
looking both ways.

No one looks at her—yet.
Shadows grow longer.

No one looks away—yet.
Across the street

unemployed men wait on a stoop
for the day-labor truck.

An old woman is crossing
to the other side where evening shadows

are longer than buildings are tall.

SUNSET

Rounded black rocks
jutting up in the blue bay,
polished smooth by wave
after wave,
for some reason in twos
everywhere
and the clocked and red
setting sun's pink light:
all of it is nature whispering
in wet, groaning language.
I listen carefully
for the meaning not in its words
but for what is not said.

MORNINGSIDE

Sunny and breezy already
this morning
morningside of the house
poor drainage but we got pink
and purple trees in bloom.
Black vulture circling above.
Coyote brush seeds on the wind.
Gray hawk on limb shifty eyed.
Gold-dust tree waving limbs.
Bald eagle standing on post.
He takes off,
wingspan ninety inches.
Probably tagged.
Heads for a bottleneck tree.
Hybrid.
Changes his mind,
goes for a bougainvillea.
And now I hear Pamela
inside moving around in the bathroom.
I go into the kitchen
and start the coffee.

TWO FACES

Face of sorrow
and face of contentment!—one upright,
another upside down.
And in that village under a noon sky,
it was too hot for anybody
to walk about in the open, even in
the narrow and cobbled passageways:
just a village street. And when he was younger
his face reflected in the streetcar window,
just as he stepped up
onto the moving vehicle. He looked
this way, knowing what he saw, and
with the church steeple behind him,
on a cloudy yet sunny day. What a face
of sorrow and expectation!
He is like and unlike his father,
they say—his father,
a thoughtful man—hand to chin,
unlike himself—hand to cheek.
And the big dreamy sad eyes
of father. Fact—it's unknown who
photographed him, white gloves
and all. But he was never like that,
white gloves and such. Much of his time
was spent in his studio with a view
of the garden, his big easel near the window,
empty bottles all about.
Just another example
of his divided self—the studio
up the hill and the apartment
in town where after all no one
wanted him, yet he kept going,
even with the village boys
throwing rocks at him,
he kept going.

THE YOUNG DOCTOR (1916)

He smiles and nods
as he drives by,
thinking perhaps soon
she will be pregnant
coming to me,
but he's wrong.
He sees a long line
of pregnant women
packed like fish
in a net bursting out
the seams of their dresses.
Ah. Give me a cup
of tea and a back rub.
Blood slime cupids cherubs, no thanks.
Give me trees losing their leaves.
I'm okay. I pay the iceman,
and he brings ice into the dark house,
inserts the block of it
into the icebox,
while church bells go *dang! dang!*
scaring the mice.
"Then again" as the fish man's nag
comes towing an old wagon
of trout, I turn about
to see who's driving by,
and I'm beginning to think he is
driving out of his way
maybe at least a mile
just to smile at me.
But no, that's crazy.
Against distant thunder
I watch my trout of many blues
being wrapped in trodden newspaper
and blundered by shaky hands.
And I understand.

LAST LIGHT

First time she saw him she was sold.
He was sitting in his rocker,
sleeping on the front porch.
What a mess, what a blessing. Now
in the evening she lights candles,
the red light lights her face gold.
In the morning the table on the terrace
is set for lunch and a delirious breeze
from the singing sea whines
over the wine glasses. And
she is often dressed in her white dress.
And I think she may be
that same woman
who walks in the park,
dark and mysterious,
with tears rimming her eyes. And
he's not by age defeated yet,
not yet,
he says my tall tall girl,
bends down
and applies ointment to her feet,
and she patiently sews buttons
back on, and reads brimming books.
And from where still on the porch
he sits now looking in my direction,
the dark farm houses
in the middle distance
glow in slow slow last light.
She sits now on the top step
in front of him and says,
back then you lifted me
from the assembly line
of an indifferent world.
I love you.

DOCTOR OF THE PLAGUE

What you can't see is the hallway,
the open window
looking out onto the canal,
and what you can't hear
is the fast talk of people
on the sidewalk below.
The one that looked most like me
I didn't like, didn't frame.
They pose too—these women
wearing the mask
of the Doctor of the Plague.
It's the same pose—I'm holding
a drawing pad, and she's light Madonna
holding a dark infant.
Naked, he holds onto his mother
with one arm and reaches down
to an older child, a brother perhaps,
and touches his shoulder.
These are the things you do know,
even when you can't see them.
The touch is discovery,
wonderment,
a test.
The place? a place that places you
back where you came from.
The blessing of the open window
is that it is not a mirror.

CHAIRS

In our house we use chairs as tables.
Look at the armchair filled with books,
a back brace, Target plastic bag, an empty frame.
It's where things go
a stopping place.
And this canvas chair unfolded
and left by the door.
At the moment it is empty
and looking lonely without my raincoat
and gloves,
my baseball cap and flashlight.
You get the picture.
I stare at its emptiness.
I'm doing it here.
And here in the kitchen
anything you want easy access to
goes on the steps of the stool.
And there is another place now
for the chair
long in the corner of the living room.
It's out in the garage
and cold to the touch
but filled with boxes.
And I can't remember what is in those boxes.
Only the love couch in the living room
remains empty,
empty except for throw pillows.
I throw them down
before I sit down in the corner
of the love couch,
yet I know they belong there more than I.

SUPPER CLUB BLUES

The curtain rose to us all,
and on stage secretly

from beneath half-closed eyelids
she scanned us the crowd

looking to see what she could see.
And what did she hope or fear to see,

wild excitement, eyebrows lifted, disgust?
We are a many-headed beast

even in the rustle of our fine fabric.
We're eating as she sings.

The restaurant is beyond control.
The waiter polite keeps coming back

like Europe emerging from the Middle Ages,
to discover we still need nothing.

And the singer takes her song like a knuckle
and twists a handkerchief around it.

She pounds the crowd
and its noise with the fist of her voice.

Three minutes. Shame on us.
Our rudeness,

clapping to a performance
we haven't heard.

And the curtain falls.

NIGHT DRIVING AND DAYDREAMING

At the zoo he fed the black rhino—a creature
of the woodlands of southeastern Africa.
That was his job.
He was not a trucker,
but he had constant thoughts
of trucks, long trucks moving rapidly
down the highway at night. And she
slept in her clothes with her backside bare,
dreaming of the spotted pony
nursing its colt. Horses?
He never hauled horses. Only things
he could lift one by one.
The monkeys grinned at him.
Church bells rang for him.
And when he pulled over to take a nap,
he dreamed of those kids years ago
on the school bench,
himself among them,
leaning forward, trying to understand
what the strange teacher was writing
about animals—tigers, lions,
sea lions—on the blackboard
while the truck in his pocket
made more sense
than all the boring words
about life
said to be wild and endangered.

IT'S RAINING IN THE LAKE

If the sun shines
while it's raining,
the devil is beating his wife,
he alcoholic, she defenseless.
That's what we said when we were children.
But was the combination
of rain and sun symbolic
of something gone wrong in nature?
Everything remembered,
even recorded, is receding
away from life and light.
And on the other side of the lake,
we have our own absence
in all its drabness thrown back to us
like an echo from an unknown place
from the hidden presence
we call seeing: seeing something
we can press a finger upon
feeling its sponginess,
the illusion of its weight.

EAST LANSING, MICHIGAN
Sept. 10th

There was no warning.
Rising from his rest
the dog bit the man's leg,
did it quietly,
then returned to his spot
on the front lawn to rest.
A solitary taproot
grows into a green bush
on which years later
a naked girl one day hangs
a wet bra to dry.
But the next morning
the dog's owner came into the man's room
carrying a tray containing croissants
and a pot of coffee,
and said, *quick! Turn on the TV,*
airplanes are flying
into the World Trade Center,
and the man knew then
that as fast as he would ever recover
from one season or reason
there would be no warning
from where the dog
or the airplane would come.
As fast as one plant dies another grows.
The man is now a seedling
just starting from the roots
of 9/11
to grow again—but into what?

VIEW FROM A BLUFF

I see a tiny bird in flight
perhaps a wren,
just a dot on the sky,
lifting itself higher
and higher on the air
above a cluster of pine
tall and dark
under a low-hanging bed
of clouds lumpy and black
as the backs of caves
closed then and now
a thousand years.
The wren is headed where rain is falling
in the far distance,
and she passes through a middle distance
aiming for a small city
where colonial slaves
white and black
are marched through its streets
to jeering crowds
and the smoke rising from it
also tells us where we are.
Something of the earth
is giving birth to itself.

DOGS

The text, this,
can't read itself.
A mouth opens with
clogged tongue
yet loosely stuck out.
See dog sniffing
a sign along earth's bed
traveling growth and gravel.
A goose on a woman's head
desperately looks about.
And there is your temple of tears
with plenty of space
laced around it roughly,
designed so you won't forget
how important
what you don't know is
and how unimportant you are.
Everywhere spears *unthrown*.
Dogs everywhere, everywhere.
Dogs climbing steep paths,
searching for anything,
anything the nose finds,
anything you may have lost.

BLACK SNAKE BLUES

Huts and houses, left and right.
Growth and gravel.
I can hear out of sight
both the nearby lake
and the wind over the lake.
Your world is titled, swaying.
These wilted flowers
here in your house are no longer vulnerable.
A country-woman with one sock on
and the other hanging in her hand.
My memory of you.
You sit on her bedside,
gazing out the sun-drenched window
at the early morning. Like a blade of light,
a black snake with a thick head
comes up from his hole
and into your Garden,
and I hear someone singing
Crawling Black Snake Blues.
You sit on the bench counting ants,
miles of them. You are naked.
Somebody is waiting in your house.
Outside, your red pony chews blue grass.
Yours, a gray stone house
stuck beneath a big gray roof.
Somebody is waiting in that house,
waiting for your arrival.
On the roof a giant black chimney.
It really defines the sky
against which it stands.
In that other distance, a seaside
and sailboats and sea,
tipping under force of constant wind
with everything flapping and flying.
Three tiny people on the bridge waving.
White boat in the inlet, sails waving.

Rolling yellow meadow.
Tossed clouds over that purple range.
I'm outside walking your yard.
Everything here deeply rooted.
Mid-afternoon, orange glows yellow.
Nothing stays the same.
A profusion. Rose bushes.
A strange girl walks by in tears.
The buckeye stands by itself
like nothing else.

A BELLY FULL OF ACID

His red and yellow wings
are the wings of a wild bird
from the caves of an ancient nightmare.
Green snake eyes.
Damaged horns above the eyes.
Flaming black hair surrounds the horns, and
his belly sags over
his gold-plated belt.
Dressed in bright chicken feathers,
he speaks through the beak of a hawk.
He dances in a circle.
He's groaning and whimpering.
He is dancing around and around.
He is whining and singing.
His feathers are falling.
He lowers his head
to run his horns into something there
only he can see.
A cloud of dust follows his feet.
A flame dances in the palm of his hand.
He is eating the flame.
The flame is eating him.

SICKERT

The naked woman who sits there posing
for the painting of a nude
sitting on the side of a bed
in a shabby room is a real woman,
whose skin, given the chance, will reflect light,
and the heavy curves of her breasts and hips
and thighs will also embrace light.
Even through your burnt umber
and raw sienna
I can smell her comforting woman smell,
and I share her grief.

COPYING

I deeply despise rules, institutions, etc. In
short, I'm looking for something other than
dogmas . . .

—Van Gogh to Bernard, Letter, 1888

The storm in the city had passed,
and Adrian and I walked through the park,
I a little in the lead,
talking over my shoulder.
I need to rest, he said. His bad knee.
The question was is it any longer necessary
to copy the great masters.
Adrian said not many art schools
still insist on it. Rules, rules· a lot to shoulder.
The trees were dripping wet
and our shoes were soaking.
Out on the highway and in the byway,
we heard the splash of speeding traffic.
Frankie says it's useful to him, I said,
just as Adrian's dog Doug caught up.
Yeah, Adrian said, I guess, but it's
just talk, and talk is not good for art.
So, I don't know, ask my dog.
I said, talk to me dog. Is there a rule?
Doug stopped and barked up at my face,
just like talking. Did it three times.

THE STARRY NIGHT

From my bed I saw through the window
the four dimensions of the night
with a sky full of stars, swirling, spinning, tumbling
stars set in the distance
by the tall black-green cypresses
in our backyard, and I briefly understood
what we painters mean when we debate space
and its shape. Part of me in lust rose up
from the bed to get a closer look
by sailing out the window
into the night sky over the railroad track,
flying above 5th Street and over the church steeple,
on to downtown Davis
and over by the train station,
but up close I lost the shape of space
because the stars consumed me
with their overwhelming presence,
and I became part of their dust.

BAD NUDES

We are a roundtable of painters.
We're talking about how to get around
the usual perception of common objects.
Ed says what he tries to do
is get his personal response to the motif
onto the surface. Win says, I have no idea
what that means. I live by the sea
and that takes courage. It's dangerous,
but out there, I know what the four corners
of space really are. What do you know,
living in the city. Joan says, I want the viewer
to feel my whole body even if it's a tree,
as long as there is no emptiness.
George says, I love emptiness.
Barney, he has a different take.
Space, he says, you can feel
without living by the sea.
Barney, he lives in the woods.
Lots of trees and rocks. Sort of Cezanne.
Jack, now there is another story.
You guys are talking about space
like you know what it is.
What you're really talking about
are pictures versus portraits.
If it's not a picture, it's a portrait.
Albert says a portrait is something you paint
that the sitter is not going to like.
Then, like Degas,
you are disinclined to change it.
Roth says space is nothing
but the place where the subject takes place,
it can be my bedroom or backyard.
My back is to the wall of bad nudes
dancing in a silly forest.

I turn to the picture
and say what would Hans make of this.
And that gets the laugh we all need.

DIFFICULT POSE

For Euan

1.

Her back is to me.
She's standing on one leg
with the other raised
and stretched as straight as possible
and with her whole upper body turned
to look back over her left shoulder
so that I see her face,
and both arms are held out at right angles
like a bird about to take off.

2.

Ah! The long Egyptian curve of her spine,
the prominence of her shoulder blades,
the curve of the buttocks,
with the overhead light
creating just the right shadow,
but the poor girl is in pain, suffering.

3.

The stretched out body,
bent, twisted, curved.
She'll refuse to come back,
but what beautiful static rhythm,
like that of tree limbs in winter
or the simple geometry of a single flower
in a whisky bottle,
or a blue steel rod casting a shadow
on a highly sculpted pear
whose each square inch of surface
reflects a different color of pear-color,
but the poor girl is in pain.
I know she won't come back,
and I'll have to finish this one from imagination.

OPEN SESSION

In the studio there is always the question
of temperature
because the naked model has to stay just right
in her nakedness,
and the rest of us have to find ways to adjust,
therefore the issue of seasons
is a matter of concern. In the summer
when she does not need her little electric heater,
and her mouth and eyes and nostrils
and ears and breasts and hands and feet
are not too cold or not too hot,
we on the other hand—depending
on which one of us
you are talking about—have to adjust
up or down.
In summer usually down—but we survive.
Now, fall is even more problematic
because here in northern California
one day might come in at eighty
and the next at fifty-five. You see
the problem for all,
even the model—especially the model.
And winter. Winter is the worst
for the model. She must have her little heater
going during all poses,
three minutes, ten minutes, twenty minutes,
the hour ones. Most of us wear sweaters
or even jackets. And then there is the problem
of keeping our hands warm.
The owner of the studio,
of course, wants to save on the expense
of energy, so he rarely turns on the thermostat.
Money like the seasons is an issue.
We each contribute ten dollars
to pay the model. If twenty of us show up

she does pretty well, but if only five or six of us
come to these Saturday morning sessions
she's almost wasted her time.

WHEN THE MODEL DOES NOT SHOW

What do artists do
when the model does not show?
The artist in charge calls her.
She says, oh shit! I forgot
or I'm sorry I had a death in the family,
or I'm not feeling well, this morning
I woke with the whole left side
of my body completely paralyzed,
or somebody stole my car
or somebody stole my bike
or somebody stole my shoes
or somebody robbed my apartment
and I'm waiting for the police right now
or my cat is sick
or my dog ran away and I'm worried
because he's missed two of his shots
or my monkey got out of the cage
and somebody just called from across town
saying they found him
with my phone number on his collar.

Then the artists say, oh well,
and stand around
talking with each other
about how some models are so dependable,
and others, well, you get the picture.
They also start looking around the studio
at paintings and drawings on the walls
as though they've never seen them before
and at those left drying on easels.
They make a few more
awkward stabs at conversation.
Then one by one
or in twos
they start packing up their supplies,

thinking about the rest of the day
and how it is going to be,
wondering if this is a bad sign,
that one thing after another
will be a disappointment,
and they start getting ready to leave
but somebody had already made coffee
so a few of them stay to finish their coffee
or to have a second cup
and ask each other
about mutual friends
they haven't seen in a long time.

PLEIN AIR

Look at Powell Street
with the trolley tracks
and the traffic jams
and the teeming crowds of tourists
and little motorbikes scooting about.
Oh, I know what the French had in mind.
Pasture with cows.
Beach house by the sea.
Hush of underbrush
where ducks suddenly shoot up
from the thicket. Last day of fall.
Sky full of dramatic clouds.
Last of the snow.
Rain over wheatfield.
Late afternoon sun
already out of sight
behind trees in the distance
and sky blazing with indirect light.
A drawbridge, a canal.
And Arles—one must not forget Arles.
Winter hills yellow and black.
Twilight on tall crop purple-green
with a touch of white light.
Midday shower in the yellow countryside.
Golden wheat harvest, no crows.
At water's edge,
empty boat slapping mossy rocks.
Summer at the beach with bathers.
And more bathers,
bathers at a stream,
bathers pretending they're near a stream.
Golden autumn.
Poppy field under blue sky.
Mountain stream
with snow-capped mountains in the distance.

But what about Powell Street,
with its griminess and noise
and trolleys and crowds of tourists
and pollution with diesel fumes
billowing out of buses.
Is this not also Nature?
Who will set up an easel here,
who will defend Powell Street?

ACKNOWLEDGMENTS

These poems appeared originally in the following publications:

"Two Faces." *Conjunctions* 41 (2003): 119.

"Three," "Night Driving and Daydreaming," "Patience," and "My Corner." *The Heritage Series of Black Poetry 1962-1975*, edited by Lauri Ramey and Paul Breman. Aldershot, Hampshire, U.K.: Ashgate, 2008.

"All of Us." *Witness* 18, no. 2 (2003): 143.

"A Belly Full of Acid." *A Folger Poetry Broadside*. Series 1976. © 1976 by Clarence Major [January 5, 1976].

"The Young Doctor (1916)." *Conversation Pieces: Poems That Talk to Other Poems*, edited by Kurt Brown and Harold Schechter. New York: Alfred A. Knopf, 2007.